The Dance Student Training Handbook

FOR DANCE INSTRUCTORS, PARENTS, AND STUDENTS

By Teresa Hill-Putnam

This handbook was created for Dance Instructors, Parents, and Students as a guideline of what skills need to be taught at each level of dance training. It is a great way for instructors, parents, and students to ensure that students learn the proper skills necessary for success.

This handbook can be used by dance instructors when teaching and choreographing routines for their dancers. The checklists will allow them to choose steps for their students within the proper level of training.

This handbook can be used as a practice guide for students and will allow them to be able to visually see what steps they still need to learn. It will help parents and students keep track of the progress being made.

Proper dance training is necessary for students to learn the correct technique in each style of dance. This handbook is **not** intended to take the place of proper dance training. The steps listed within this handbook serve as a basic guideline and should be arranged in fun combinations for students to practice and perform. Instead of teaching proper technique, many dance studios today just focus on teaching specific choreography and "tricks" for recital dances and/or competitions. By not teaching proper dance technique, students are often left with huge holes in their training. They have only a small skill set of steps they can do and they are more prone to injury. Dance is a progressive art form consisting of hundreds of steps and the mastery of proper technique. There is a specific order in which students should learn each dance step. Each level of dance builds on the one before and allows students to correctly develop their muscles, as they build their technique. While Ballet is the basis of all dance forms, learning a variety of styles helps a dancer become more well-rounded and more employable if they choose to become a professional dancer.

I have spent over 35 years perfecting these dance skills checklists for my students. I have successfully instructed thousands of students over the years and have enjoyed watching them shine!

Ballet Skills Checklist

What Your Ballet Student Needs To Know

Ballet Levels 1-5

FOR BALLET INSTRUCTORS, PARENTS, AND STUDENTS

BY TERESA HILL-PUTNAM

Spotlight Performers ©   www.spotlightperformers.com

Ballet Level 1 Skills Checklist

Butterfly stretch
Straddle stretch
Hamstring stretch
Coupe' and Passe' while lying on back
Sickle & Bevel ("naughty toes" and "nice toes")

<u>At the Barre</u>
Plie' (to bend)
Tendu (to stretch)
Releve' (to rise)
Passe'(to pass)
Coupe' (to cut-wrap foot around ankle)
E'chappe' (to escape)
Arabesque

<u>In the Center</u>
1st Position
2nd Position
3rd Position
4th Position
5th Position
Port de Bras (dance of the arms)
Saute' (to jump)
Ballet Walk (toe, heel, toe, heel…)
Ballet Run (run on balls of feet)
Chasse' (to chase)
Hop on two feet
Hop on one foot
March
Step together (Glissade prep)
Skip
Walk on demi pointe (tippi toes)
Twirl (preparation for Pirouette)
Leap (Grand jete' prep)
Following the Leader
Balancing item on head
Walking on a line or balance beam
Jumping Jacks
Reverance (Curtsy)

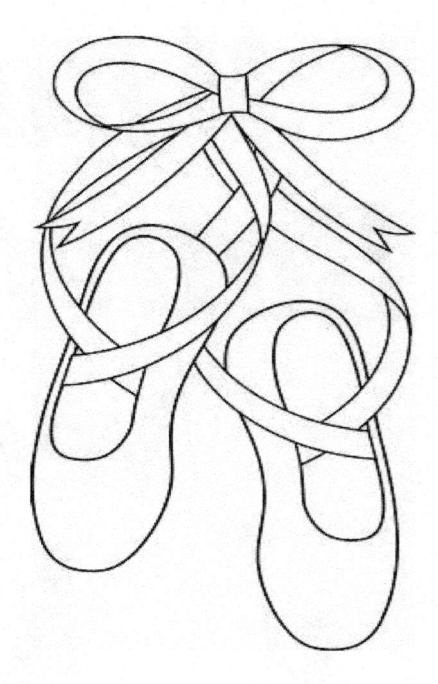

Coloring Pages and Flashcards are available (Perfect for students ages 2-6 years old!)
To order, visit www.spotlightperformers.com.

Ballet Level 2 Skills Checklist
(Students should be able to understand and master Level 1 skills)

Butterfly stretch
Straddle stretch
Hamstring stretch
Frog stretch
Coupe' and Passe' while lying on back
Point and flex (Parallel and Turned out)

At the Barre
Demi plie' (in 1st and 2nd position)
Grand plie' (in 1st and 2nd position)
Cambre' (to arch)
Tendu (to stretch)
Releve' (to rise)-with balance
Rond de jambe en dehors (outward circle from front to the back)
Retire' with balance (to Retire)-Ballet and Jazz positions
De'gage' (to disengage)
Frappe' (to strike)
Passe' (to pass)
Coupe' (to cut-wrap foot around ankle)
Attitude
De'veloppe' (to develop)
Grand battement (big beating stretch)
Sous-sus (under-over)
E'chappe' (to escape)

Adagio-Slow
5 positions of feet with arms added
1st port de bras (dance of the arms)
3rd port de bras
4th port de bras
5th port de bras
Right and Left identification
Pirouette (single)
Bourre'e (stuffed)
Balance' (a rocking waltz)

(Ballet Level 2 Continued)

<u>Allegro-Fast</u>
Saute' (to jump)
Changement (to change)
Glissade (to glide)
Pas de chat (step of the cat)
Grapevine
Jazz Square

<u>Across the Floor</u>
Ballet Walk
Ballet Run
Chasse' (to chase)
Hop on one foot
March (with a jazz passe')
Skip (forward and backwards)
Spotting
Chaine' tour (chain of turns)
Pique' (to prick)
Grand Jete' (Big leap)
Reverance (Curtsy)

Ballet Level 3 Skills Checklist
(Students should be able to understand and master Level 1 and 2 skills)

Butterfly stretch
Straddle stretch
Hamstring stretch
Frog stretch
Coupe' and Passe' while lying on back
Splits (R, L, Center)
Point and flex (Parallel and Turned out)

At the Barre
Demi plie' (in 1st, 2nd, 4th, and 5th positions)
Grand plie' (in 1st, 2nd, 4th, and 5th positions)
Cambre' (to arch)
en croix (in a cross=Front, Side, Back, Side)
Tendu en croix (to stretch)
Eleve'(to bring up) vs. Releve' (plie' and then rise)
Releve' (to rise)-with balance
Rond de jambe en dehors (outward circle of leg from front to the back)
Rond de jambe en dedans (inward circle of leg from back to front)
Retire' in releve' with balance (to retire)-Ballet and Jazz positions
Coupe' in releve' with balance (to cut)
De'gage' en croix (to disengage)
Frappe' en croix (to strike)
Passe' (to pass)
Attitude
De'veloppe' en croix (to develop)
Fondu en croix (to melt)
Grand battement en croix (big beating stretch)
Sous-sus (under-over)
E'chappe' (to escape)

Adagio-Slow
5 positions of feet and arms
1st port de bras (dance of the arms)
2nd port de bras
3rd port de bras
4th port de bras
5th port de bras

(Ballet Level 3 Continued)

Pirouette (Single)
    en dehors-outward
    en dedans-inward
Bourre'e (stuffed)
Sous-sus tour
Balance' turn (a rocking waltz)
Grapevine
Jazz Square
Pivot turn
Fankick
Hitchkick

<u>Allegro-Fast</u>
Saute' (to jump)
Changement (to change)
Glissade (to glide)
Pas de chat (step of the cat)
Petite Jete'(little leap)
Assemble' (to assemble)
Sissonne (scissors)

<u>Across the Floor</u>
Ballet Walk
Ballet Run
Chasse' (to chase)
Skip (forward, backwards, and turning)
Polka
Spotting
Chaine' turns in plie' and releve' (chain of turns)
Pique' turns (to prick)
Grand Jete' (Big leap)
Saut de chat (cat's jump)
Tour jete' (turning leap)
Saute' arabesque
Reverance (Curtsy)

Ballet Level 4 Skills Checklist
(Students should be able to understand and master Level 1, 2, & 3 skills)

Butterfly stretch
Straddle stretch
Hamstring stretch
Frog stretch
Splits (R, L, Center)
Point and flex (Parallel and Turned out)

At the Barre
Demi plie' (in 1st, 2nd, 4th, and 5th positions)
Grand plie' (in 1st, 2nd, 4th, and 5th positions)
Cambre' (to arch)
en croix (in a cross-F, S, B, S)
Tendu en croix (to stretch)
Releve' (to rise)-with balance
Rond de jambe en dehors (a terre and en l'air)
Rond de jambe en dedans (a terre and en l'air)
Retire' (to Retire)-Ballet and Jazz position in releve' with balance
Coupe'(to cut) vs Sur la Cou-de-pied (position on the next of the foot)
Coupe' (to cut) in releve' with balance
De'gage' en croix (to disengage)
Frappe' en croix - Single and double(to strike)
Passe' (to pass)
Attitude
Developpe' en croix (to develop)
Fondu en croix (to melt)
Pas de cheval (step of the horse)
Grand battement encroix (big beating stretch)
Sous-sus (under-over)
E'chappe' (to escape)

Adagio-Slow
5 positions of feet and arms
1st port de bras (dance of the arms)
2nd port de bras
3rd port de bras
4th port de bras
5th port de bras

(Ballet Level 4 Continued)

1st Arabesque
2nd Arabesque
3rd Arabesque
4th Arabesque
5th Arabesque
Pirouette (Single and Double)
    en dehors-outward
    en dedans-inward
Drag turn
Bourre'e (stuffed)
Sous-sus tour
Soutenu (to sustain)
Soutenu tour
Balance' tour (a rocking waltz)
Pas de bourre'e (stuffed- Back, Side, Front)
Grapevine
Jazz Square
Pivot turn
Fankick
Hitchkick

<u>Allegro-Fast</u>
Saute' (to jump)
Changement (to change)
Entrechecat (beating jump)
Royale (beating changement)
Glissade (to glide)
Pas de chat (step of the cat)
Petite Jete'(little leap)
Assemble' (to assemble)
Sissonne en croix (scissors)
Straddle jump

(Ballet Level 4 Continued)

<u>Across the Floor</u>
Skip (forward, backwards, and turning)
Polka
Pas de basque
Spotting
Chaine' turns continuous (chain of turns)
Pique' turns (to prick)
Tombe' (to fall)
Grand Jete' (Big leap)
Saut de chat (cat's jump)
Tour jete' with arabesque hold (turning leap)
Chasse' + Saute' arabesque
Reverance (Curtsy)

Vocabulary:
    Croise'-crossed
    En face-facing the front
    E'fface'-shaded
    E'carte'-separated
    E'paulment'-shouldering
    Devant-in the front
    Derriere-in the back, behind
    A la seconde-in the 2nd position
    En avant-forward
    En arriere-Backward
    En bas-low

Ballet Level 5 Skills Checklist
(Students should be able to understand and master Level 1,2,3, & 4 skills)

Butterfly stretch
Straddle stretch
Hamstring stretch
Frog stretch
Splits (R, L, Center)
Point and flex (Parallel and Turned out)

At the Barre
Demi plie' (in 1st, 2nd, 4th, and 5th positions)
Grand plie' (in 1st, 2nd, 4th, and 5th positions)
Cambre' (to arch)
en croix (in a cross-F, S, B, S)
Tendu en croix (to stretch)
Releve' (to rise)-with balance
Rond de jambe en dehors (a terre and en l'air at 90+ degrees)
Rond de jambe en dedans (a terre and en l'air at 90 + degrees)
Retire' (to Retire)-Ballet and Jazz position in releve' with balance
Coupe'(to cut) vs Sur la Cou-de-pied (position on the neck of the foot)
Coupe' (to cut) in releve' with balance
De'gage' en croix (to disengage)
Frappe' en croix - Single and double (to strike)
Passe' (to pass)
Attitude
De'veloppe' en croix at 90+ degrees with hold (to develop)
Arabesque with Penche'-leaning
Fondu en croix at 45 degrees and 90 degrees (to melt)
Pas de cheval (step of the horse)
Grand battement en croix (big beating stretch)
Sous-sus (under-over)
E'chappe' (to escape)

Adagio-Slow
5 positions of feet and arms
Port de bras (1-5 with body and head positions)
Arabesque (1-5 positions at 90+ degree)

(Ballet Level 5 Continued)

Pirouette (Single, Double and Triple)
    en dehors-outward
    en dedans-inward
Fouette' turns
A la seconde tour
Bourre'e (stuffed)
Sous-sus tour
Soutenu (to sustain)
Soutenu tour
Balance' tour (a rocking waltz)
Pas de bourre'e combinations (stuffed: B-S-F, F-S-B, F-S-F, and B-S-B)
Grapevine
Jazz Square
Pivot turn
Fankick
Hitchkick

Allegro-Fast
Saute' (to jump)
Changement (to change)
Entrechecat (beating jump)
Royale (beating changement)
Glissade (to glide)
Pas de chat (step of the cat)
Petite Jete' (little leap)
Assemble' (to assemble)
Sissonne en croix (scissors)
Russian -Straddle jump (toe touch)

Across the Floor
Brise' (Broken, beating)
Ballonne' (bouncing step)
Skip (forward, backwards, and turning)
Polka
Pas de basque
Spotting
Chaine' turns continuous (chain of turns)
Pique' turns- Single and Double (to prick)

(Ballet Level 5 Continued)

Drag Turn
Attitude Turn
Arabesque turn
Waltz Turns
Grand Fouette'
Tombe' (to fall)
Grand Jete' (Big leap)
Saut de chat (cat's jump)
Tour jete' with arabesque hold (turning leap)
Center Leap (large Glissade)
Chasse' + Saute' arabesque
Reverance (Curtsy)

Tap Dancing Skills Checklist

What Your Tap Student Needs To Know

Tap Dancing Levels 1-4

FOR TAP INSTRUCTORS, PARENTS, AND STUDENTS

By Teresa Hill-Putnam

Spotlight Performers© www.spotlightperformers.com

Tap Dacing Level 1 Skills Checklist

Toe
Ball
Heel
Dig
Right vs. Left
Kick
Brush
Spank
Hop on two feet
Hop on one foot

Marching (forward and backwards)
Jumping Jacks
Skip
Chasse': To chase (gallop around the room like a pony)
Step, Heel (to side, switching feet)
Step, Toe (behind, switching feet)
Brush step (moving forward)
Shuffle
Flap (pronounced "Fallap")
Ball-Change
Turn and Kick Bottom
Walk on Heels
Walk on Balls of Feet
Shuffle Step
Shuffle Hop
Shuffle Toe (behind)
Shuffle Hop Toe
Flap Step
Flap heel
Tap Run (on balls of feet)
Grapevine: Step (side), cross front, step (side), cross behind
Sugar: Twisting back and forth on the balls of the feet
Tap Curtsy (Heel to side, Toe behind)

Tap Dancing Level 2 Skills Checklist

All level 1 skills plus:

Hop step (changing feet)

Step vs Stomp

Stomp Hop, Step (Changing feet)

Cramp Roll (Ball, Ball, Heel, Heel)

Shuffle (to the Front and to the Side)

Shuffle Step (changing Feet)

Shuffle Toe step (changing feet)

Shuffle hop step (changing feet)

Flap (to the Front and to the Side)

Flap walks (moving Forward and Backwards)

Flap heel (changing feet)

Flap Step (changing feet)

Flap hop

Flap hop step (changing feet)

Flap run

Ball-change

Kick Ball-change

Brush Ball-change

Shuffle Ball-change

Flap Ball-change

Buffalo: step (R), Shuffle (L), Leap to other foot (pick up R foot in front)

(Tap Dancing Level 2 Checklist Continued)

Chaine' Turns: Chain of turns (slowly)

Jazz Passe'

Timestep #1: Stomp, Hop, Step, Flap, Step (slowly)

Timestep #2: Stomp, Hop, Flap, Flap, Step (slowly)

Maxi Ford: Step, Shuffle, Leap, Toe

Essence: Step ball-change (in front), step ball-change (in front), step ball-change (in front), ball-change, ball-change

Charleston: Step, kick front, step, kick back

Cincinnati: Brush back, hop, shuffle step

Grapevine with Flaps

Lindy (Chasse', step, ball-change)

Shirley Temple: Flap, heel, heel, brush, heel, toe, heel

Waltz Clog: Step, shuffle ball-change

Double Waltz Clog: Flap, shuffle ball-change

Suzie Q: Step forward with foot turned in, step, twist foot to turn out

Tap Dancing Level 3 Skills Checklist

All level 1 and 2 Skills Plus:

Shuffle (to the Front, to the Side, and to the Back)

Irish Shuffle: A shuffle that crosses in the front

Shuffle Ball-change Shuffle hop, step

Irish (Shuffle Ball-change Irish Shuffle hop, step)

Flap (to the Front, to the Side, and to the Back)

Flap heel, heel (alternating feet)

Double Buffalo (Flap, Shuffle, leap to other foot)

Double Maxi Ford (Flap, Shuffle, Leap, Toe)

Buffalo Turn (Single and double)

Maxi Ford Turn (Single and double)

Timestep #1 and #2 (faster and turning)

Timestep #3- Stomp hop Shuffle step, Flap, step

Repeater: Backwards Flap (1 foot at a time)

Pullback: Backwards Flap (both feet together)

Wing prep: sideways shuffle step (1 foot at a time)

Wing: sideways shuffle step (both feet together)

Single pirouette (with Jazz Passe')

Scuff: brush forward with heel

5 count Riff (Toe scuff, heel, heel step)

Tap Dancing Level 4 Skills Checklist

All Level 1-3 Skills plus:

Single foot Pullbacks

Syncopated Wings

Timestep #3 (faster and with turn)

Timestep #4 (Stomp hop shuffle step, shuffle step, flap, step)

Timestep #4 Changing feet (Stomp hop shuffle step, shuffle flap, step)

Timestep #4 (with Turn)

Timestep # 4 Changing feet (with Turn)

Traveling Time Step: Shuffle Ball-change Ball-change hop shuffle step, shuffle step, shuffle step

Shirley Temple (with turn)

Barrel Turn

Double Pirouette (with Jazz Passe')

Chaine' Turns (with flaps)

12 count Riff
(Toe, scuff, heel, heel, brush, heel, toe, heel, scuff, heel, heel step)

Tip Timesteps

Wing Timesteps

Tip Wing Timesteps

Paradiddle: Heel, spank, step, heel

Jazz Dance Skills Checklist

What Your Jazz Student Needs To Know

Jazz Dance Levels 1-4

FOR JAZZ INSTRUCTORS, PARENTS, AND STUDENTS

By Teresa Hill-Putnam

Spotlight Performers ©   www.spotlightperformers.com

Jazz Dance Skills Checklist Level 1

<u>Stretching</u>
Butterfly
Hamstring
Straddle

<u>Isolation exercises</u>
Head isolation
Shoulder isolation
Rib isolation
Hip isolation
Body Rolls

Plie': To bend (Parallel, 1st, and 2nd positions)
Releve': To rise (Parallel and in 1st position)
Tendu: To stretch
De'gage': To disengage
Ballet Passe': To pass (turned out)
Jazz Passe': To pass (parallel)
Arabesque
Port de Bras: Dance of the arms
Shoulder Shimmy
Jazz Hands
Jazz Square
Grapevine
Jazz Walks (walk on the beat)
Lunges
Pirouette preparation
Pirouette
Kick Ball-Change
Pivot turn
Hitchkick
Pas de bourre'e: Stuffed (3 steps-Back, Side, lunge)

(Jazz Dance Skills Checklist Level 1 Continued)

Chasse': To chase
Skip
Grand Battement: Big Beat (kick)
Fankick
Saute': To jump
"Spotting"
Chaine' turn: A chain of turns
Pique': To prick
Grand Jete': Big leap
Glissade: To glide (preparation for Center Leap)
Coffee Grinder
Curtsy or Bow

Jazz Dance Skills Checklist Level 2

All Jazz Dance Level 1 Skills, Plus:

Tendu (en croix: in the shape of a cross- Front, Side, Back, Side)
De'gage' (en croix)
Rond de jambe: Circle of the leg
Ballet Passe' (with Retire' balance)
Jazz Passe' (with Retire' balance)
Attitude
De'veloppe': To develop
Pas de bourre'e (Turning)
6 step Pas de bourre'e
Jazz Walks:
    Walk on the Beat
    Drag Walk
    Passe' Walk
    Walk with De'veloppe' (Pas de cheval: Step of the horse)
    Running on the Beat
Lindy: Chasse', Ball-change
Charleston: Step, kick front, step, kick back
Rodger Rabbit
Jazz Square (with Jump)
Single Pirouette (en dehour and en dedan)
Kick Ball-Change, Pirouette
Skip (forward, backwards, and turning)
Polka: Chasse' + skip
Chaine' Turns (faster and with variation)
Pique' Turn
Attitude Turn
Saute' Arabesque
Tour Jete': Turning Leap
Saut de chat: The Cat's Jump
Center leap

Jazz Dance Skills Checklist Level 3

All Jazz Level 1 & 2 Skills, Plus:

Ballet Passe' in Releve' (with balance)
Jazz Passe' in Releve' (with balance)
Rond de jamb (en lair)
De'veloppe' (en croix- at 90 degrees or higher)
Penche': leaning
Heel Stretch: Leg hold
Tilt: A leg extension with body tilted to make a line
Pas de bourre'e combinations (with and without turns)
Single Pirouette (with hold in Retire')
Double Pirouette
Layout
Battement with layout
Fan kick with layout
Chaine' turn combinations
Pique' turn combinations
Attitude turn combinations
Arabesque turn
A la seconde turn (basic): with leg extended out to the side
Fouette' turn prep: to whip
Axel
Chaine', fan-kick
Chaine', Calypso (fan-kick leap)
Barrel turn
Russian (Straddle jump)
C- jump
Stag leap: Grand jete' with front leg bent under
Scorpion leap: Grand jete' with back leg bent up toward head
Pump leap: Grand jete' with back leg kicking out mid leap
Turning Center Leap
Back leap

Jazz Dance Skills Checklist Level 4

All Jazz Skills Level 1, 2, and 3, Plus:

Conditioning:
- Splits
- Crunchies
- Push ups (regular, right, left, crab, bridge)
- "Fire hydrant" kicks

Attitude turn (in all directions)
Double pirouette (with Retire' hold)
Triple pirouette
Illusion-a backward rond de jambe (in penche') while pivoting
Six step pas de bourre'e, pirouette
Fouette' turns
A la seconde turns
Pencil turn
Leg Hold Turn
Double Pique' turns
Progressive turn combinations (Chaine' turns, Pique' turns, Attitude turns, axles, etc.)
Leap combinations (grand jete', saute de chat, center leaps, switch leap, tour jete', back leap, scorpion, stag, calypso, etc.)
Switch leap: A leap where legs switch mid leap
Switch Center Leap

Acro-Gymnastics Skills Checklist

What Your Acro-Gymnastics Student Needs To Know

Acro-Gymnastics Levels 1-5

FOR INSTRUCTORS, PARENTS, AND STUDENTS

By Teresa Hill-Putnam

Spotlight Performers ©   www.spotlightperformers.com

Acro-Gymnastics Skills Level 1

Stretching
Point and Flex
Butterfly
Hamstring
Straddle
Crab
Bridge
Donut
Cheerio
Superman (on floor and on yoga ball)
Frog Stretch

On Tumbling Mat
Bear Walk
Crab Walk
Log Roll
Forward Roll (Somersault)
Backward Roll
Front Straddle Roll
Back Straddle Roll
Donkey Kick
Handstand (against the wall)
Cartwheel

Dance Steps
(All Acro-Gymnastics students benefit from proper Ballet and Jazz Training. This is a list of the minimum basic dance skills they should know.)
Plie': To Bend
Tendu: To Stretch
Releve': To rise
Jazz Passe'
Ballet Passe'
Arabesque

(Acro-Gymnastics Skills Level 1 Continued)

Port de Bras: Dance of the Arms
Pirouette
Saute': To jump
Hurdle
Tuck Jump
Grand Battement (front, side, back): Big Beat (kick)
Hitch kick
Jazz Square
Grapevine
Pique': To prick
Chaine' Turn: Chain of turns
Chasse': To chase
Skip (Forward and Backward)
Grand Jete': Big Leap

Acro-Gymnastics Skills Level 2

All Acro-Gymnastics Skills Level 1, plus:

<u>Warm-up</u>
Splits (Right, Left, and Center)
Tripod to headstand
Bridge push-ups
Bridge warm ups (lifting hands and feet-alternating)
Handstand Push-ups (against the wall)
Handstand tricks (against the wall)

<u>On Tumbling Mat</u>
Split roll
Crab to Bear Rolls
"Spider-walk" in a Bridge across the mat
Backbend
Extension (Backward roll to handstand)
Handstand hold
Handstand to Forward Roll
Handstand to Split
Handstand to bridge
Two handed Cartwheel (facing front)
Two handed Cartwheel (facing sideways)
One handed Cartwheel
Running Cartwheel
Chaine' Turn + Cartwheel
Round off
Shoulder roll
Run and Hurdle

<u>Dance Steps</u>
Developpe' (front, side, back): To develop
Fan Kick
"Russian" (Toe Touch Jump)

(Acro-Gymnastics Skills Level 2 Continued)

C-Jump
Pique' Turn
Skip (Turning)
Saut de Chat leap: Cat step
Tour jete': Turning leap

Acro-Gymnastics Skills Level 3

All Acro-Gymnastics Skills Levels 1 and 2, Plus:

Conditioning:
- Crunchies
- Push ups (regular, right, left, crab, bridge)
- "Fire hydrant" kicks

On Tumbling Mat
- Bear to Bridge Rolls
- Kip Up
- Dive Roll
- Front Limber
- Back Limber
- Tik-Tok (in place)
- "Press" to handstand
- Reach-over (one handed) Cartwheel
- Dive Cartwheel
- Running Cartwheel (with pickup)
- Round-off
- One handed Roundoff
- Reach over Roundoff
- Dive Roundoff
- Running Roundoff

Dance Steps
- Heel Stretch (Leg hold)
- Attitude turn
- Center leap
- Barrel Turn

Acro -Gymnastics Skills Level 4

All Acro-Gymnastics Skills Levels 1-3, Plus:

On Tumbling Mat
Turning Headstand
Walking Handstand
Turning Handstand
Front Walk-over
Back Walk-over
Walking Tik-toks (Forward and Backward)
Valdez (from sitting to back-walkover)
Tinsica (Cartwheel into a front walkover)
Elbow Cartwheel
Elbow Roundoff
Partner Cartwheel
Aerial Prep
Front handspring
Backhandspring Prep

Dance Steps
Heel Stretch Turn (Leg hold)
Illusion
Back Leap
Scorpion leap

Acro-Gymnastics Skills Level 5

All Acro-Gymnastics Skills Levels 1-4, Plus:

<u>On Tumbling Mat</u>
One Handed Front Walkover
One Handed Back Walkover
Elbow Front Walkover
Elbow Back Walkover
Dive Front Walkover
Scissor Walkovers (front and back)
Aerial: No handed cartwheel
Brandy : Aerial roundoff
Standing Back Handspring
Round-off Back Handspring
Walkout
Standing Back Tuck
Roundoff Back Tuck
Roundoff Back Handspring, Back Tuck
Front Aerial
Pee Wee/Rolling Tinsica (Rolling Cartwheel Walkover)

<u>Dance Steps</u>
Calypso (fan kick leap)
Switch leap

Is the Cost of Dance Training Worth It?

Remember: Parents of dance students do not only pay for dance lessons, they pay for so much more!

Dance training teaches dancers to:

- Make and accomplish their goals
- Work hard
- Develop their talents
- Never give up
- Solve problems
- Overcome obstacles
- Shine in the spotlight
- Deal with disappointment
- Make lifelong friendships
- Learn self-discipline
- Take proper care of themselves
- Work as a team with others
- Learn grace, poise, and balance
- Appreciate and enjoy dance as an art form
- Improve memorization
- Be physically fit
- Increase stamina
- Improvise
- Be a good student in other areas of life

Parents do not only pay for dance lessons, they pay for the many wonderful opportunities that dance provides. Dance is not just about movement, it is a way of life!

HOW PARENTS CAN HELP THEIR DANCER BE SUCCESSFUL

- Support and encourage your dancer! Let them know that you value their hard work. Developing a talent requires an investment of energy, time, and money. It is a commitment for both the dancer and the parent.

- The more commitment your dancer puts into their craft, the more they will learn and the further they will go. The more skills they develop (ie: Dancing, Singing, Acting, Tumbling, and Public Speaking), the more opportunities that will be available to them. Practice makes progress. A dancer that practices more often will develop more advanced skills and will be given more opportunities.

- Help your dancer look professional for classes, auditions, meetings, rehearsals, events, and performances (appropriate clothing, well groomed, and hair combed.) Teach them to have good manners and how to act in a professional environment. You only get one chance to make that first impression.

- Communication is the key! Make sure you communicate appropriately with everyone on their team (teachers, coaches, studio owners, agents, managers, school, etc). Check your phone and/or email regularly so you do not miss any important information.

- Make sure your dancer is well prepared for classes, rehearsals, performances, and jobs. Children who prove themselves to be responsible and hard working are often given extra opportunities/recognition.

- ALWAYS be on time. It is better to be 30 minutes early, than 1 minute late.

- Keep a positive attitude. Gossip, negativity, disrespect, and lack of professionalism will quickly end further opportunities.

- Nurture, encourage, and respect your child. Avoid comparing them to other children. EVERY child has the right to make mistakes, learn, and grow. Help prepare your child for big emotions when they don't get the role they desire. Help to keep them motivated. Remember, every professional started out as a beginner.

- Remember that every role/performance is important, no matter how big or small!

"A BEGINNING dancer knows nothing.

An INTERMEDIATE dancer knows everything!
(They think they are too good to dance with beginners)

A "HOTSHOT" dancer thinks they are too good to dance with anyone.

An ADVANCED dancer dances everything… especially with beginners."

-Richard Crum

"A small child at dancing class might never become a professional dancer- but the courtesies and disciplines, as well as the joy in movement, will touch their lives forever!"

-Helen Thompson

Practice makes progress.

100 WAYS TO BOOST SELF-CONFIDENCE IN CHILDREN

1. Notice them.
2. Smile.
3. Acknowledge their feelings.
4. Ask them about themselves.
5. Look in their eyes when you talk to them.
6. Listen to them.
7. Giggle together.
8. Tell them that their feelings are important.
9. Set boundaries that keep them safe.
10. Be honest.
11. Hug them often.
12. Give them one-on-one attention.
13. Listen to their stories
14. Notice when they are acting differently.
15. Play with them.
16. Present options when they seek your counsel.
17. Stay with them when they are afraid.
18. Suggest better behaviors when they act out.
19. Delight in their discoveries
20. Share their excitement.
21. Allow them to take the lead and follow them.
22. Give them space when they need it.
23. Contribute to their collections.
24. Discuss their dreams and nightmares.
25. Laugh at their jokes.
26. Kneel or squat so you're at their eye level.
27. Answer their questions.
28. Tell them how terrific they are!
29. Create a tradition with them and keep it.
30. Hold hands during a walk.
31. Apologize when you do something wrong.
32. Keep the promises you make.
33. Hug, wave, and smile when you part.
34. Point out what you like about them.
35. Give them lots of compliments.
36. Catch them doing something right.
37. Take them out for ice cream.
38. Ask for their opinion.
39. Tell them how much you like being with them.
40. Be excited when you see them.
41. Praise more and criticize less.
42. Let them act their age
43. Give them a special nickname.
44. Marvel at what they can do.
45. Tell them how proud you are of them.
46. Pamper them.
47. Applaud their successes.
48. Tell them stories in which they're the Hero.
49. Believe in them.

50. Nurture them with good food, kind words, and great fun.
51. Be flexible.
52. Delight in their uniqueness.
53. Help them learn from their mistakes.
54. Include them in conversations.
55. Respect them.
56. Visit their schools, classes, performances, concerts, games, and other events.
57. Understand when they have a difficult day.
58. Help them make good choices.
59. Respect the choices they make
60. Appreciate their individuality.
61. Be silly together.
62. Make time to be with them and write it on your calendar.
63. Help them learn something new.
64. Tolerate their interruptions.
65. Trust them.
66. Share a secret.
67. Create a safe and open environment
68. Get involved.
69. Encourage them to help others.
70. Tackle new tasks together.
71. Help them take a stand and stand with them.
72. Daydream with them.
73. Do what they like to do.
74. Make decisions together.
75. Magnify their magnificence.
76. Encourage them to think big.
77. Welcome their suggestions.
78. Be sincere.
79. Tell them what you expect of them.
80. Introduce them to new people.
81. Introduce them to new experiences.
82. Share meals together.
83. Expect their best; don't expect perfection.
84. Empower them to be themselves.
85. Encourage them to be a good friend
86. Read together.
87. Say "yes" a lot.
88. Enjoy your time together.
89. Tell them about yourself.
90. Let them solve most of their own problems.
91. Help them become an expert at something.
92. Help them learn to deal with conflicts.
93. Get to know their friends. Let them have parties and other social engagements.
94. Be consistent.
95. Accept them as they are.
96. Inspire their creativity.
97. Make yourself available
98. Use your ears more than your mouth.
99. Let them tell you how they feel.
100. Love them, no matter what!

"A hundred years from now, it will not matter what kind of house I lived in, what kind of clothes I wore, or how much money I had… but the world may be different because I was important in the life of a child!"

-Forest E Witcraft, Teacher and Scholar

5 Rules for learning:

Be quiet

Listen

Follow directions

Do your best

Have fun!

Behind every dancer is a dance teacher standing in the wings with a stomach full of butterflies and a heart full of pride!

There is no proper time frame for learning. All students learn at their own pace.

Never forget:
You are **TERRIFIC!**

"I wasn't born to JUST TEACH. I was born to INSPIRE others, to CHANGE PEOPLE, and to NEVER GIVE UP… Even when faced with challenges that seem impossible."

-Raj Kumar

After owning and directing a large Performing Arts School for over 35 years, Teresa Hill-Putnam is now a Performance Coach and Motivational Speaker. She also offers Master Classes and Private Coaching.

Teresa lives and works in Los Angeles, California.
She is a proud mother and "Grammy."
When not working, Teresa loves to drink coffee, eat chocolate, and travel.

Teresa's other books include:
The Show Must Go On
From One Show To the Next
The Script of Life
And
My Daily Pep Talk

Teresa also has a podcast series called
Overcoming Obstacles Through Positive Thinking

For more information or to schedule a Master Class or Private Coaching Session, please contact Teresa at www.spotlightperformers.com

Printed in Great Britain
by Amazon